ANY OLD IRON

The Story of the Yorkshire Farm Machinery
Preservation Society

by E. Blanchard

Hutton Press
1984

List of Illustrations

*The Publishers and Author wish to thank the 'Hull Daily Mail' for permission
to use photographs on page 16 (16hp hot bulb) and page 18 (Councillor Flynn).*

Printed by B.A. Press, 18 North Bar Within, Beverley, North Humberside.
Telephone 0482 882232
©1984. Hutton Press Ltd., 130 Canada Drive, Cherry Burton, Beverley,
North Humberside, HU17 7SB.
ISBN 0 907033 18 0

Introduction

Being born of farming stock, raised in a farming community, and being in agriculture in one capacity or another all my life, it was inevitable that, when a society to collect and preserve old and obsolete farm machinery, implements, and small tools was suggested, I should become involved. The ultimate objective was to establish a museum of this long out-dated equipment, but at that time, we had little knowledge of the cost of such a project or the labour it entailed.

However, we continued to build up the collection, although our hopes of a museum diminished as quickly as the collection increased. But, after eighteen years of dedicated hard work, our prayers were at last answered, and the Yorkshire Museum of Farming became a reality.

So, if those of you who read this and visit our museum, get as much pleasure from viewing the many hundreds of items displayed there, as my colleagues and I got from collecting and restoring them, then those eighteen years have not been wasted, and we could ask for no greater reward.

The success of any voluntary society, whatever its objectives, depends entirely on the enthusiasm and support of its members, and in this our society was indeed fortunate. Although our membership was very widely scattered, there were many living within reasonable distance who were always ready to help in any way they could, some by donating items to improve the collection, others by providing transport, a very valuable contribution indeed.

Regrettably, a number of our early supporters were denied the opportunity of seeing their efforts reach fruition. I know how they would have enjoyed watching it gradually nearing completion, and I wish to express my own personal tribute to those named below, who in our early days helped in so many ways when help was so urgently needed.

The Lord Hotham	Dalton Holme, Nr. Beverley
The Lord Halifax	Garrowby House, Bishop Wilton, York
Mr. W. Dent	Cammerton Farm, Thorngumbald
Mr. Stanley Martinson	Main Road, Wyton. Late of Humbleton House
Mr. John Martinson	Bellasize Farm, Gilberdyke

Mr. M. D. Thackray	Castle Howard Drive, Malton
Mr. Charles Hopkinson	The Mount, Malton
Mr. John Conner	Fowler Bungalow, Boynton, Bridlington
Mr. Dick Preston	Potto, Northallerton
Mr. Wm. Newton	Wistow Common, Selby
Mr. C. E. Alden	Foggathorpe, Selby
Mr. H. Burley	Market Weighton
Mr. W. H. Coupland	Market Weighton
Mr. R. Burley	Holme on Spalding Moor
Mr. Sidney Atkinson	Station Road, Eastrington
Mr. Robin Sawyer	Goodmanham, Market Weighton
Mr. Henry Reffold	Walk House, Kiplingcotes
Mr. George Reffold	Preston, Nr. Hull
Mr. Bernard Hall	Etton, Nr. Beverley
Mr. Ted Stocks	Wood Lane, Beverley
Mrs. Mary Stocks	Wood Lane, Beverley
Mrs. Alice Scruton	7 Highgate, Beverley
Mrs. H. M. Scruton	Lairgate, Beverley
Mr. A. T. Heald	The Old Hall, Atwick
Mr. Jim Jackson	White House, Keyingham
Mr. Charles Turnbull	Beverley
Mr. Ted Darley	Hemingborough, Nr. Selby
Mr. Harry Wroot	11 The Balk, Pocklington
Mr. W. B. Morrell	Chairman, Yorkshire Folk Park Trust
Mr. Jack Hoe	Minster Towers, Beverley
Mr. J. M. Webster	Far Farm, Kexby, York

E. Blanchard

About the Author

Edwin (Ted) Blanchard was born near Selby in 1905. He went into farming in 1926 during the times of the depression, and worked on farms till January, 1941, when he joined the staff of the West Riding Agricultural Executive Committee in Skipton. In 1956 he was transferred to Beverley and retired in the area in 1970.

Mr. Blanchard has been connected with the Yorkshire Farm Machinery Preservation Society since 1965.

CHAPTER ONE

Any Old Iron

It is many years since the late Harry Champion took the world of entertainment by storm with that famous old song. Like so many others, before and since, it enjoyed tremendous popularity for quite some time, then gradually faded into oblivion. Today it is heard only on very rare occasions when some old-timer, in a fit of nostalgia, asks for it to be played on some radio programme.

The wind of change was blowing even then, and nowhere did it blow harder than on agriculture. The methods which, in the days of our fathers were in everyday use, are now seldom — if ever — employed. The machinery and implements which served them so well for so long have now vanished for ever, and the pairs of horses, plodding patiently along at about two-and-a-half miles per hour, drawing a single furrow plough turning over about one acre per day, have now been replaced by huge tractors — noisy, smelly contraptions in a multitude of colours, drawing five or six furrows at more than twice the speed of the horses.

Farming, like everything else, had to change with the times. Two World Wars, during which food production was of paramount importance if we were to survive, made certain that to continue using the methods, implements, etc., used for generations by our forefathers could only result in farming becoming no longer viable.

These thoughts had been in our minds for some time, but they were highlighted when early in 1965 students at Longcroft School, Beverley, brought small items of old and obsolete farm tools and equipment to school in connection with their studies. Mr. H. E. Kirk, who at that time taught rural science there, conceived the idea of forming a society for the purpose of collecting and preserving a representative collection of old and obsolete farm machinery, implements, and small tools, with the establishment of a permanent museum where such a collection could be displayed as our ultimate objective.

A small number of enthusiasts in the Beverley area, under the chairmanship of Mr. Richard Marginson, a well-known Beverley farmer, met regularly for over a year and, with the spadework completed, a public meeting was held in Agriculture House, Beverley, on 27th October, 1966, and the East Riding Agricultural Machinery Preservation Society was officially formed, with Mr. Kirk as secretary and a committee of seven members for the purpose of trying to put our ideas into operation.

The meeting was well attended, and there was obviously a good deal of interest throughout the county in the project, but there were a number of problems to be overcome.

First, in order of seniority, came finance, without which nothing can succeed. To collect, restore, house, and display a collection such as we hoped eventually to acquire would need money — lots of money. It was decided that membership would be open to all who were prepared to subscribe one pound per annum, whether they wished to become actively involved in the society's activities or not.

At last we had made a start, even if our membership was, at that time, pitifully small, and during the following months our farming friends supported us nobly, donating many interesting and unusual objects, and we soon had a varied and quite extensive collection. Some pieces were almost two hundred years old, some of them indescribably crude and certainly irreplaceable — all of them interesting and historically valuable.

The next and possibly the most daunting problem was accommodation, or the lack of it. We already had the foundation of a fascinating collection, but nowhere to put it. Our friends generously agreed to store it for us until we could make our own arrangements, and indeed some of them are still doing just that.

We had boundless enthusiasm, but no money — certainly nothing like the amount needed even for a very small beginning. We had a number of members ready, willing, able, and indeed anxious to begin work on restoration in their spare time, but no workshop facilities to enable them to do so, and after two years or so it became very obvious that if the society was to survive, something would have to be done. We needed help, urgently and quickly.

Letters to all the local rural councils produced nothing more than a few words of encouragement and a few, very few and very small, donations. Indeed, some of them could not be bothered to reply.

During that time our chairman, Mr. Richard Marginson, became Chairman of the East Riding branch of the National Farmer's Union, and with so many demands on his time, he asked to be relieved of his appointment. So, in 1967, I found myself elected chairman — a position I had certainly not anticipated, but which I enjoyed immensely for sixteen years.

The society was by then registered as a charity.

During the Summer of 1967 the Yorkshire Agricultural Society generously allowed us an area at the Great Yorkshire Show at Harrogate, where we could exhibit some of our collection, and some of our members who had transport facilities were equally generous in providing us with free transport.

On the first day of the show we had no sooner got our stand organised and set out when the BBC television unit descended upon us. The resulting TV programme was seen all over the county, and provided us with an excellent bit of free advertising, as well as a substantial increase in our membership.

The main exhibit on this stand was a fifty-year-old Titan tractor, loaned to us by Mr. Horstine Farmery, one of our founder members. This was the first of many busy but very enjoyable Great Yorkshire Shows, where our members came regularly every year to see us and brought new members with them, and it became the highlight of our summer season for many years. The Yorkshire Agricultural Society supported us magnificently, and their support was very much appreciated, for without it there would have been little — if any — progress, and indeed our very survival would have been extremely doubtful.

Whether it was the Yorkshire tenacity of purpose or our failure to recognise and admit defeat I know not, but whatever the reason, we refused to be discouraged and carried on.

After the first two years or so had been spent in trying to put the society onto a solid foundation, we realised that our title in its original form was rather too much of a mouthful. A motion to amend it to the 'Yorkshire Farm Machinery Preservation Society' was carried unanimously, and we continued to be known by that title until the Annual General Meeting in February, 1983, when the society was reconstituted and renamed.

CHAPTER TWO

A Glimmer of Hope at Last

About the end of 1968, when we were almost at our wits' end to decide where to look next, a suggestion was put forward by Mr. Joe Spencer, now resident in Pieter-Maritsburg, South Africa, that perhaps one of our stately homes which were open to the public might be interested enough to allow us space to exhibit some of our collection, and here we found success at last.

After making approaches to several people, we contacted the owners of Burton Constable Hall, at Sproatly, near Hull, Mr. and Mrs. J. R. Chichester Constable. They showed immediate interest in the idea, and agreed to allow us the use of part of the stable block and another building adjoining which could accommodate six tractors, and so, in Spring, 1969, our first permanent public exhibition opened.

It was, of necessity, on a small scale, but at least we had at last got people coming to see what we had got, and in this we were greatly indebted to Mr. Harry Gibson, of Marton, who owned a number of old tractors and let us have four on loan, which added variety to the exhibit and helped to fill it up.

In those early days Mr. Gibson helped us a great deal, for in addition to the loan of the tractors, he also provided transport to collect items and bring them to Burton Constable, and in those days when our collection was only beginning to take shape and our funds were lamentably low, this was of tremendous help. Indeed, we could not have managed without the help of, not only Mr. Gibson, but also the late Stanley Martinson, Mr. John Elgy, Mr. Tom Musgrave, Mr. Leslie Hight, the late Mr. L. Brooksbank, Mr. Richard Hall, and several others who spared no effort to help us along when our funds were insufficient to meet this kind of expense.

For a number of years the society attended local shows, rallies, and similar events whenever possible, exhibiting a few stationary engines and various small tools and implements, in addition to a sales stall where we had on sale various items such as lettered pens, car badges, lapel badges, car stickers, etc. For several years we also had for sale an extensive range of very attractive souvenir items in brass and bronze, ranging from horse brasses to solid brass caravans complete with a horse, and these helped to boost our funds quite a bit.

We began with what could only be described as a shoe-string budget, but before our purpose had been achieved our annual turnover had reached

£2,500. Not much, it is true, but this was achieved by three or four — often less — enthusiasts who worked hard for nothing to keep our society on its wheels, in the hope that what began as a dream might someday become a reality. And now, at last, it has.

In 1970, after having taken over part of the stable block at Burton Constable for display purpose, it was decided that during the winter months while the hall and grounds were closed to the public, the first Sunday in each month should be a working day, so that volunteers who were willing to help with restoration work would find the buildings open for them to do so. This idea was received with enthusiasm, and the first Sunday saw ten volunteers spend a very useful day there.

The following month numbers dropped to six, the next month it was four, and although we continued with the idea for several years, enthusiasm faded to virtually nothing, and after some ten years or so — during which I had to be there for the day, whatever the weather, doing all I could single-handed — the idea was abandoned.

There was no shortage of work to be done, but the formation of an East Yorkshire branch of the National Vintage Tractor Club had the effect, unintentionally I am sure, of encouraging many of our members to get an old tractor of their own and restore it to showroom condition at home, rather than travel to Burton Constable to work voluntarily on machines which could never be their own.

Although this was a quite understandable development, it did nothing to help us, and we were all the more grateful to those members who continued to support us financially by keeping their subscriptions going. Invitations from both the East Riding and the West Riding branches to take our sales stall to their rallies were gladly accepted and helped to raise a little more revenue to keep us going.

Over the years the society's membership fluctuated a great deal, and numbers varied from anything between one hundred and forty and three hundred. Sometimes subscriptions were overlooked for some years and then paid up to date, even on occasions for some years in advance, but our membership secretary for many years, Mr. Tom Burley, kept the situation well in hand, and did not allow those who were inclined to overlook payment to continue in arrears for too long.

In addition to being membership secretary, he also helped me to produce a newsletter about three times a year, so that members could be kept informed of events during the year. He is still a capable model maker and mechanic, and carried out for us many repairs to items which were not too big for either his workshop or my car. It is fairly safe to say that he was, and still is, capable of making almost anything out of nothing, and over the years he has helped us out of many an awkward situation by making parts which, being very old, were otherwise unobtainable. He thus made it possible to preserve for ever implements and machines which would otherwise have ended up on the scrap heap.

Another early member was Tom Theakston of Driffield, a machinery instructor at the East Riding College of Agriculture, who organised some of his students into a students' club which spent one night a week working on whatever old machinery we took down there, in their workshops and under his supervision. A good deal of useful work was carried out for us there, including the complete overhaul of an Edlington sail reaper dating from 1880, which had been donated in our early days by Messrs. Swift Bros. of Wawne.

With visitors to Burton Constable throughout the summer of around 35,000 to 40,000, many of whom showed a great interest in our society, our work and our exhibits, our membership increased, and, in addition, we had space in which to carry out restoraton work under cover during the winter months when the hall was closed to the public. It is an indisputable fact that, but for the support of Mr. and Mrs. Chichester Constable, the society could never have reached its objective.

This beautiful hall, dating from 1570, the spacious grounds, and the various functions which took place there attracted a great many visitors who visited our display along with the others, and we were — and still are — extremely grateful for the opportunities provided for us in such a beautiful setting.

Burton Constable Hall

CHAPTER THREE

Searching, Ever Searching

All this time we continued to collect suitable additions to the collection, among them a rather unusual binder which only used one canvas instead of the usual three. It has now been restored by our friend Mr. W. Shillito, and it is being stored by him until we have room for it. This was donated by the late Mr. Shepherd, of Carnaby, and was collected on a trailer towed behind my car, with assistance in loading from Ken Scruton and one or two others.

Several years earlier I had occasion to visit Cotness Hall Farm, Laxton, a large arable farm situated almost on the banks of the River Ouse, near Howden. There I discovered a piece of machinery known variously as a horse wheel, gin race, or mill race. It was sitting, rusty and derelict, where it had sat for more than a hundred years. Except for the poles to which the horses were yoked it was complete, and the straw chopper — or choppy-cutter as they were known in the East Riding — which it used to drive was also there, albeit in rather poor condition.

It was a type of machine rarely seen nowadays, and as it lay there almost overgrown by nettles, there was nothing to indicate its rather tragic history. Here, on this very spot, in about 1905, Joseph Robinson, a worker employed on this farm, was fatally injured when his foot was trapped in the revolving cog-wheel while he was driving the horses.

Mr. L. Sweeting, who with his sons farms this and the next farm, was of the opinion that the machine should go to some museum for preservation, and when I became involved in the formation of our society some years later, he gladly agreed to let us have it. Some time later it was removed by myself and Charles Cawood, but while being transported to Burton Constable for re-erection, the framework was accidently broken. This necessitated a welding operation for which we had to wait an awfully long time, but at last it was completed and has been re-erected.

Embossed on the cast iron framework was the name 'I. Drury, Maker, Reedness'. My curiosity was aroused, and I went to Reedness to see whether I could learn anything more about the machine.

Reedness is a small farming village on the south bank of the River Ouse, and it was here, in the early 1840's, that John Drury started in the business as a maker of farm implements. In addition to horse wheels of various sizes, he also made a complete range of the horse-drawn implements of the day —

Horse Wheel or Gin Race

ploughs, scrufflers, harrows, seed and turnip drills, etc., as well as various hand tools. By now a cast iron plate bearing his name and the date 1849 will have been placed in position on the wall of the building in which he worked.

The business evidently prospered, for it was not until the early 1940's that the production of implements ceased after one hundred years of unbroken activity. The family then concentrated on farming. Good as they undoubtedly were, these country craftsmen could hardly be expected to meet the competition provided by the bigger companies with their mass production methods and more sophisticated equipment, and gradually they disappeared, having laid the foundation of what is now a gigantic and highly prosperous industry.

When John Drury started his business in the 1840's he could hardly have foreseen the tremendous developments which were to take place in the years ahead, for this was the time when history was being made. Indeed it was here, on these premises, in a shed where a garage now stands, that the first self-binder ever to be seen in these parts was stored. When harvest arrived, it was delivered to a local farm to start work, and a few days later still, it was in pieces, broken up and destroyed by the local workers, who feared that this new machine would rob them of their jobs and their livelihood.

Now, six generations and one hundred and forty years later, the buildings and farm are still in the hands of the Drury family. The foundry has gone, and a new bungalow has been erected in its place. The old forge, now a firewood store, has little to remind one of its original function except the half-buried anvil, and the rows of nails in the beams above, whereon hung the stock of hand-made horseshoes.

The machine shop which adjoins is also used for storage. Behind the pile of fertiliser sacks is the lathe, which was in use for over a hundred years, and the shafting with its many varying sizes of pulleys for driving the lathe is still in position on the wall. Above it hang two wooden patterns, used in casting, one for the giant mill race wheel and the other for the base plate in the form of a large cross.

Near the door the joiner's bench is still in place, with its collection of grooving planes on the shelf above, but the workshop, alas, is now silent. No longer do the horses plod gently round in circles to provide power to drive the machinery, no longer does smoke bellow from the squat, blackened chimney, nor does the anvil ring under the mighty hammer. The song is ended, but the melody lingers on.

*   *   *

It was in 1899 that William Shillito, a young man of about twenty years of age, took over Preston Fields Farm, at Preston in the Holderness area of East Yorkshire. In common with many others, capital was none too plentiful, but hard work and the application of a sound knowledge of farming principles, coupled with the enthusiasm of youth, saw him prosper so that in 1895 he was in a position to order a new farm wagon from each of the two wagon builders in the village, Messrs. Fewster and Messrs. Healas.

Drawn by two horses, each of these wagons was capable of carrying three tons or more, and they spent the whole of their working lives on this farm, carrying its produce to and from the railway station or into the city, the hay and grain crops from the fields to the farmstead during harvest, and generally fulfilling the multitude of uses and misuses to which farm wagons of those days were subjected.

The outbreak of the First World War, with men and horses being needed for military service, compelled farmers to adopt, albeit unwillingly, a certain amount of mechanisation if they were to survive. As tractors gradually replaced horses, wagons originally designed to be horse-drawn could be seen hitched two at a time behind a tractor and carrying loads and travelling at speeds for which they were never intended.

When the effects of this misuse became evident, the wagons were replaced by trailers designed specifically for use behind tractors. They were mounted on pneumatic tyres and were capable of carrying greater loads at greater speeds. The two wagons had served their owner well, but now they must be discarded as of no further use, and for several years they remained under the cartshed which had always been their home.

When, in 1966, the Yorkshire Farm Machinery Preservation Society was formed, Mr. William Shillito, Jnr., who had inherited the farm on the death of his father, donated the two wagons to the society and generously

13

continued to store them until we had space in which to keep them and sufficient funds to ensure their restoration.

During the spring of 1977 the first of these two wagons, the Fewster, was taken to the workshop of Messrs. P. H. Sissons & Son of Beswick, near Driffield, who carried out its restoration.

As could be expected of a family business with a reputation for wagon building covering several generations, the Fewster returned, as good as new and resplendant in its original colours, in time to make its appearance at the Great Yorkshire Show at Harrogate, where it was greatly admired. The following year the other wagon, the Healas, was also restored by Messrs. Sissons, and both are now in excellent condition and likely to be for many years.

It is interesting to note that when new in 1895, the Fewster wagon cost £25 and the Healas slightly more at about £30. The cost of their restoration was some twenty times that amount, but we were helped by a grant from the museum and art gallery services.

What a wagon of that type would cost now, were one obtainable, I dare not ask, but we are extremely grateful to Mr. Shillito for two splendid additions to our collection.

★   ★   ★

Yorkshire Wolds Wagon, built 1895

Soon after this we were approached by Mr. John Allman, of North Frodingham, whose father, the last of several generations of village blacksmiths, had recently passed away, leaving his smithy just as he had always used it. Mr. Allman offered the whole of the contents of the shop to us on condition that they could be kept together.

This most generous offer was accepted, provided that things could stay as they were until we could erect a place to put them in. All the contents have now been collected and are at the museum at Murton awaiting re-erection. Before long, we hope, visitors will be able to see a country smithy just as it used to be, and we are grateful to Mr. Allman for a magnificent gift.

★   ★   ★

A year or so later we attended the Castle Howard Steam Fair, as we usually did, and there we were visited by Mr. Dick Hodgson, of Manor Farm, Kirklevington, Cleveland, who offered us a wonderful old barn thresher, made in about 1850 and driven by an overhead horse wheel, which unfortunately was missing. It had not been used for many years, but was in good condition considering its age.

I visited the farm to inspect the machine and made sure we could handle its removal. After having it photographed in detail to facilitate its re-erection, a gang of about six of us went there one Saturday, dismantled it, carried it out of the barn, loaded it onto a lorry, and were just ready to start for home at nine o'clock, with a journey before us of some seventy-five miles or so.

As the museum at Murton continues to develop we shall be looking for a place to re-erect it, for there are very few of these machines left. Our thanks to Mr. Hodgson and his son for a rare and interesting exhibit.

★   ★   ★

Among the many visitors to our first display at the Great Yorkshire Show at Harrogate was Mr. C. E. Alden, of Foggathorpe, who offered to donate a 16 h.p. Hornsby hot bulb oil engine, which used to drive all the machinery in their joiner's shop. Unfortunately, it had suffered damage by frost, and a crack the whole length of the cylinder block had been temporarily repaired by clamping a piece of wood along the crack.

The offer was accepted with thanks, especially as he undertook to keep it there for us until we had a place to put it. It was some years before we could do that, but we decided to move it when we learned that other collectors were pestering Mr. Alden to let them have it.

Having arranged a day for its collection, we went down in the morning to find Mr. Alden busy removing the roof from the building. At lunch time John Elgy arrived with his wagon, closely followed by Mr. J. Marrables from Shiptonthorpe with his heavy-duty recovery vehicle, and within an

16hp Hot Bulb Oil Engine

hour the engine was hoisted bodily through the roof and onto the wagon, to be roped and transported to Mr. Elgy's farm at Bainton.

Next day it was moved to Burton Constable, where another good friend, Mr. L. V. Brooksbank from Hedon, was there with his mightly mobile crane to lift it from the wagon and set it down on a bed of concrete.

A week or two later our secretary, Ted Kirk, assisted by David Scott, erected a wooden building over it with a large glass window to make viewing easier. It made an interesting item for the Yorkshire Television news that night, and an equally interesting item for the visitors to look at.

★　　　★　　　★

In the spring of 1970 the Illingworth family from Birdsall emigrated to Australia, giving up all their farms except one in the Birdsall and Howsham areas in order to take up farming 'down under'. Before their farm sale John, the eldest son, donated two tractors to our society, a 1942 W.9, and a 1952 Farmall M, both in good running order.

As our activities at that time were regarded as agricultural operations, we were able to licence and insure the W.9 as an agricultural tractor, and having had a tractor trailer donated, we were able to do our own haulage provided it was not for 'hire or reward'. However, at that time, legislation was being enacted to make the fitting of safety cabs or roll bars on tractors compulsory. Road taxes and insurances were also being drastically increased, making the use of this outfit on the roads no longer a viable proposition. So, with regret, we had to abandon its use, except on land. Along with several other engines, it was driven in the parade at the annual traction engine rally until they were all moved to Murton, where they can still be seen.

★   ★   ★

Among the early members of our society was the then Mayor of Beverley Urban District Council, Councillor Harry Flynn who, although unable to take an active part in our activities, was always on the lookout for anything he thought would interest us.

While on a camping holiday in Cornwall in 1970, Councillor Flynn discovered an old single row turnip seed drill, believed to be between 100 and 150 years old, standing derelict and rusty in an outhouse near where they were camping.

The farmer/owner was approached by Councillor Flynn, and was quite pleased to donate the drill to the society, but there still remained the problem of getting it back to Yorkshire, since their only available form of transport was bicycles.

Never a man to allow a little thing like that to bother him, he returned to Beverley on his bicycle when his holiday ended, borrowed a pick-up truck, and on the Saturday returned to Cornwall, picked up the old drill, and returned to Beverley on the Sunday. On the Monday morning I arranged to meet him at Burton Constable Hall, where he presented the drill to Mr. Chichester Constable and myself on behalf of the society. A few necessary repairs were later carried out by Ken Scruton, who also painted it, and it can now be seen in the museum at Murton.

Members who are prepared to make a journey of nine hundred miles at their own expense and in their own time are not very easy to find, nor are those who restored the drill, and our gratitude was suitably expressed by Mr. Chichester Constable and myself.

★   ★   ★

Additions to our collection come about by various means, but the most important thing is that they do come, and when, in the autumn of 1979, I heard of a most unusual and very old Yorkshire farm wagon, I lost no time in getting down to New Village Farm, Newport, to see it.

I was not disappointed. In spite of the fact that we already had two, in showroom condition, this one was something different in that it was on

Turnip Seed Drill

straked wheels instead of the usual hoops. It is the only such wagon I have ever seen in East Yorkshire and only the second I have seen anywhere.

As may be expected after many years standing outside in all weathers, its condition is somewhat delicate, but now that we have got it under cover we can decide at our leisure whether complete restoration is practicable, or whether we shall have to be satisfied with the wheels only.

In any case, it is an extremely rare and interesting item, and we are grateful to Mr. W. E. Underwood for donating it to the society.

★   ★   ★

Some years ago I heard that an old-established butcher in Bridlington, Mr. Hart, was retiring from business and disposing of all his equipment. This included an 'animal hoist', a large wooden pulley on a wooden shafting, with a long rope wound round the pulley and two shorter ropes, each with a hook at the end, upon which the hind legs of the slaughtered beast were hung. It was then hoisted up to facilitate dressing the carcase.

This hoist was sitting on top of the beams in the slaughter house roof, and Mr. Hart very kindly donated it to our society, complete with the problem of how we were to get it down. However, with a cab and trailer and several helpers, we went to collect it. After studying for some time how to do it, one of our members, Mr. Eric Wood of Dalton Holme, came up with the answer.

The pulley was turned up to its maximum height, then the hooks which normally held the animal's legs were fastened to the beams, and the bearings upon which it turned were dismantled. The ratchets were then released and the whole apparatus was lowered to the ground by allowing it to slowly run down its own ropes, steadied by means of the rope round the large pulley.

Easy when you know how, isn't it? Getting it through the door presented another minor problem, but it was done, loaded up on the trailer and transported to Burton Constable. It can be seen now, re-erected, in the livestock building at the museum at Murton.

★   ★   ★

'Mystifier' Crop Sprayer

Collecting and restoring old and obsolete bits of farm machinery, implements and hand tools could not really be regarded as everyone's cup of tea, but to those with a genuine and active interest in the subject it is indeed a fascinating and absorbing hobby. The discovery in some remote corner, overgrown with nettles or briars, of some long forgotten gem of equipment which two hundred or so years ago was in general use on our farms, is something we are always hoping for. Occasionally it does happen, and when it does it is a tremendous thrill. But it does not end there. Next comes the many hours of hard work, the stripping down, cleaning, repairing, painting and rebuilding.

Once the work is completed, there is the satisfaction of knowing that we have preserved for future generations something that, but for our efforts, they might never have known existed, let alone how it was used.

Farmall Model H Tractor

CHAPTER FOUR
Great Oaks from Little Acorns Grow

During the winter of 1976 an article appeared in the press publishing some details of our work, including the fact that we were fast outgrowing our available accommodation and were looking for more extensive premises which would enable us to get most of our ever increasing collection under cover. The article caught the eye of Mr. Eric Pocklington, a partner in the York Livestock Centre, and also Messrs. R. H. English & Son of Pocklington. Mr. Pocklington then approached me with the suggestion that perhaps a building might be erected at the livestock centre.

Accompanied by Mr. J. F. Stephenson, another partner in the livestock centre, Mr. Pocklington came over to Burton Constable to see what was in the collection. Both showed great interest and both joined the society as members.

At that time we envisaged no more than a large building where we could set out the collection in a manner which made viewing easy for visitors, but even a plain building costs money, which had be be found somehow.

After another year, a proposal by Mr. James Stephenson resulted in the formation of a museum sub-committee to explore ways and means of setting up a museum. This committee consisted of Messrs. John Leak, E. T. Harland, W. Dale, J. F. Stephenson, who undertook the duties of secretary, and myself. The well-known broadcaster and curator of the Yorkshire Museum, Mr. Michael Clegg, was also co-opted in an advisory capacity.

Several very useful meetings were held. The York Livestock Centre agreed to provide a site adjoining the centre, but still there was the question of finance. The cost of buildings, etc., was rising continually, and any means of raising the amount needed appeared beyond our reach.

At this point we approached the trustees of the Yorkshire Folk Park Trust, who held in trust a large sum of money for just such a purpose. The trust had been established several years before by the late Doctor Morrell, but the scheme then proposed never materialised, and the money remained in trust. A meeting was arranged between the trustees and the society's museum committee, at which we outlined what we had in mind and appealed for their help. In addition to displaying a definite interest, they also came up with some sound practical advice.

We were advised to commission a feasibility study on the project, and it was recommended that we employ Mr. James Gardner, a London consultant who, among other things, had designed the QE2, the Battersea pleasure gardens, the National Museum in Israel, a large museum in Holland, and also one in America. The cost of this study, £1,500, was to be shared between ourselves, the trustees of the Folk Park trust, and the museum and art gallery services for Yorkshire and Humberside.

Mr. Gardner, whose ability to sketch the items in the collection speedily and accurately really amazed me, examined the collection, visited a number of museums in the area to ascertain the possible visitor potential, and then submitted his report.

He suggested we should try to tell the story of the development of agriculture from as far back as we could and illustrate this with items from the collection, placing the remainder on display in reserve accommodation. After some consideration his recommendation was approved.

After a good deal of thought, the trustees of the Folk Park Trust decided to support us, and we were notified that they were to donate £90,000 towards the museum, subject to certain conditions, i.e.:

That we could raise a similar amount from the public sector; that we would permit the project to be examined by a museum consultant of their own choice; that the trust would be granted equal representation on the museum management committee.

Eventually we were able to meet these conditions, and a company was formed, to be known as the Yorkshire Museum of Farming Ltd. The company was to be limited by guarantee and registered as a charity. A committee of management was formed with each of the participating bodies having equal representation. At last we were on our way, but our problems were by no means at an end.

At the Annual General Meeting held at the Livestock Centre on 8th February, 1977, Mr. Charles Cawood proposed that the office of treasurer be filled by one of our own members, since professional services were expensive and unsatisfactory and did not provide sufficient information. This was agreed, but there was a marked reluctance among the members to accept the post. After a lengthy discussion, we at last had a volunteer and after a formal proposal by Mr. Cawood he was duly elected.

A week after this meeting I received a letter from Mr. Ted Kirk stating that on doctor's orders he was obliged, with extreme regret, to resign immediately from the position of secretary, having been taken ill on the way home from the meeting.

Under the circumstances, we had no option but to accept this, with much regret, since Mr. Kirk had been an extremely capable and efficient secretary from the very beginning. Indeed, it was his idea to form the society in the first place. But we were left in a rather awkward position of having to find another secretary so soon after the beginning of another year. Eventually, Mr. Tony Waddingham accepted the position.

Soon after this, it became apparent that the treasurer we had elected had underestimated his responsibilities, and our financial affairs were becoming somewhat chaotic. However, having been warned, I kept a duplicate set of books. This was fortunate as it turned out, for at the next Annual General Meeting it became clear that the production of any sort of annual financial statement was quite beyond his capabilities. Some three weeks after the meeting he resigned from his post and also from the society, and the treasurer's duties continued to rest upon me until 1983, when the society was reconstituted and its title changed.

Having overcome the problems created by the unavoidable resignation of our secretary, Mr. Kirk, and our somewhat disastrous first attempt at an internal audit, the activities of the museum sub-committee increased until the volume of work made it necessary to provide an assistant to help Mr. J. F. Stephenson carry out what was beginning to look like a full-time job. Mr. M. B. Horner of Dunnington was engaged on a temporary part-time basis, and together they produced a brochure setting out the proposal, the estimated costing of the project, etc., and now things were really starting to move.

The museum sub-committee approved a motion to donate the whole of the collection owned by the preservation society to the Yorkshire Museum of Farming, on condition that a display would remain at Burton Constable for as long as Mr. Chichester Constable wished it to do so, and that the society would be represented on the museum management committee as of right. These conditions being acceptable, the motion was submitted to the general committee of the preservation society and again approved unanimously.

The motion was then put to an extra-ordinary general meeting of the preservation society, and it was again approved unanimously after a long and detailed discussion. In my opinion, it was this decision which influenced the Folk Park Trust to support the museum project, in particular their chairman, the late Mr. W. B. Morrell. This was put on a legal footing by an agreement prepared by Mr. R. A. Bellingham, the society's honorary solicitor, and agreed and signed by both parties.

Messrs. Robin Wade Design Associates were appointed designers, with Mr. John Crosby, of Boulton & Crosby, Harrogate, as architect. Upon the formation of the museum company, Mr. Bryan Horner was engaged as the full-time administrative director. It now remained to get possession of the eight-acre site which, although owned by the livestock centre, was tenanted by a local farmer who was somewhat reluctant to terminate his tenancy.

Finance was still a consideration, so a public appeal was launched by Mr. Ted Moult, the well-known farmer and broadcaster. The appeal was launched in September, 1980, in conjunction with a collective sale of farm machinery and implements. A percentage of the proceeds from the sale, in some cases all of it, was to go towards the museum appeal. Although the sale attracted a large number of buyers and spectators, the bidding was not always as brisk as we would have liked.

Meanwhile, the designers and architect were getting on with their job, and having obtained possession of the site, draining and landscaping were necessary before buildings could be erected to house the collection.

First came the conservation building. Messrs. Hares, of Bedale, were commissioned to do the job, and a very useful building emerged, with a workshop included where work was soon going ahead. Next came what we term the 'Four Seasons Galleries', which is to house the main part of the collection upstairs. On the mezzanine floor stands a pulpit, once in use in a demolished Methodist chapel, and here our first Harvest Festival was held in 1982, with the congregation literally surrounded by a variety of old and obsolete tools and equipment.

Then came the livestock building, which contains shepherds' tools, a large collection of dairy equipment, a reproduction of James Herriot's surgery, and a farrier's workshop. Alongside, at a lower level, are loose boxes for pigs, calves, cows and horses, which during the summer are turned out to graze in the paddocks adjoining.

On 15th July, 1982, the museum was opened to the public on a limited scale and for a short season in order to 'test the market'. The project appeared to be well received by the public, and 13,127 visitors came to the museum during the few weeks it was open in 1982.

In February, 1983, at the Annual General Meeting held at the York Livestock Centre, the Yorkshire Farm Machinery Preservation Society, which for eighteen years had battled against all the odds to establish a permanent museum, ceased to exist. Its title was changed to the 'Friends of the Yorkshire Museum of Farming'. The original objective now achieved, its collection was officially and legally transferred to the museum.

We who are left and who worked so hard to achieve this can feel justifiably pleased and proud that what we set out to do we have accomplished, with a little help from our friends, and we can be proud of what, as a result of our efforts over many years, shows every sign of being a popular and successful museum.

My work completed, I handed in my resignation as chairman in order to make room for some new blood in the team, and our membership secretary for many years, Mr. Tom Burley, also resigned. Now we can both sit back and watch the project grow.

During all these years we were fortunate in having the ever-present David Scott, a retired colleague from Beverley, whose help was invaluable to me in carrying out our restoration programme and who also assisted at shows and acquired additions to our collection. Almost always available, always willing to help in whatever way we wished, he was a tower of strength for a number of years until the collection was transferred to Murton, and our appreciation can never be adequately expressed.